James Payn

A New and Easy Method to Learn to Sing by Book

James Payn

A New and Easy Method to Learn to Sing by Book

ISBN/EAN: 9783744759526

Printed in Europe, USA, Canada, Australia, Japan

Cover: Foto ©Thomas Meinert / pixelio.de

More available books at **www.hansebooks.com**

A New and Easie

METHOD

To Learn to

Sing by Book:

WHEREBY

One (who hath a good *Voice* and *Ear*) may, without other help, learn to Sing true by NOTES.

Design'd chiefly for, and applied to, the promoting of PSALMODY; *and furnished with variety of* Psalm Tunes *in Parts, with* Directions *for that kind of Singing.*

LICENSED,

Jan. 29. 168 $\frac{5}{6}$.   *Rob. Midgley.*

LONDON,

Printed for *William Rogers*, at the *Sun*, againſt St. *Dunſtan's* Church in *Fleet-Street*, 1686.

To the Ingenious and Hopeful

THOMAS FOLEY,

Eldest Son of the Worshipful

THOMAS FOLEY, of *Witley*, Esq;

AND ALSO

To the Vertuous Young LADIES

LETITIA and *ANNE*,

Eldest Daughters of the Worshipful

PHILIP FOLEY, of *Prestwood*, Esq;

The AUTHOR (as an Acknowledgment
of his Obligations to that Worthy Fa-
mily, whereof these are Branches)

HUMBLY DEDICATETH

THIS

ESSAY.

THE
PREFACE.

AMONG those *Human Arts that are made use of in Divine Things, none is more immediately serviceable than* MUSIC, *which not only is admitted within the Walls of* the Church, *but also assists at the most Sacred Offices therein performed. Of what Esteem and Use in Divine Things it was of, Old among the* Jews, *the Scriptures give us account, and largely afford the Subjects and Matter of their Song: The good King, and chief Psalmist, being therein characterized with the Title of,* The Sweet Singer of Israel. *Under the Gospel, we have both the Example of our Saviour at his last Supper, and the Commands of the Apostles, for Singing; and accordingly, in all Ages since hath it been practised by Christians. The*

N4-

The Preface.

Nature and Effects of Muſic, *are ſuch as com-mend it to ſo honourable Service*; Motion, Proportion, Concord, *and* Harmony, *being the very Soul of it*, *and to excite and expreſs the beſt Affections*, *its genuine Effects.*

Of all kinds of Muſic, *that expreſs'd by* Human Voice *hath the precedence*, *as being moſt ancient and natural* Nature afords us Organs, *both to expreſs and entertain its Me-lody*; *y͏t herein, as in other caſes*, *Nature is to be perfected by Art and Induſtry.* A Ruſtic, *tho' he may have Natural Parts*, *and a Soyl for Learning*, *is yet*, *if illiterate*, *incapable of Converſe with Scholars*, *or enlarging his Know-ledge by Books* : *In like manner*, *tho' a perſon have naturally a good Voice and Ear*, *yet without ſomething of Art*, *will he be incapable of Muſical Conſort or Learning*, *more than what (as a Par-rot) he gets by rote.*

That ſo few perſons (out of Cathedrals) under-ſtand Prick-Song, a main reaſon v, the Obſcu-rity and Confuſion in the Method commonly taught, wherein the following Particulars make it a long Drudgery to attain Proficiency.

1. *A*

1. *At first fight, we have prefented a long Bead-roll of hard and ufelefs Names, to be conn'd backward and forward in the* Gam-ut.

2. *When this Drudgery is over, follows a worfe, to learn the differing Names of the Notes, according to the feveral places of* Mi, *which in each Cliff hath three feveral Stations, being one while in* B, *another while in* F *another while in* A, *the other Names* (Fa, Sol, La,) *attending its motions.*

3. *When you are paft thefe two, and can name your Notes three manner of ways, you are yet to feek for the chief thing, the Tuning of them, if you have not a Mafter at hand to lead you with his Voice or Inftrument.*

As to the Notes Names, and the Cliffs, fe the *Old* and *New ways* compared in a *Table* at the end of *Chap. IX.*

4. *A fourth Difficulty arifes from the many Cliffs, which no lefs than feven ways change the places of the Notes upon the Lines and Spaces, and makes it a moft tedious thing to be perfect in all, or but fome of them.*

The

The Preface.

The removal of these Difficulties, and thereby the Encouragement of Learners, is that which I have endeavoured in this Essay: What I have done in order thereto, I shall here give the Reader some account of.

First, as to the Gam-ut, omitting the old Names of the Notes as unnecessary, I retain only the Letters of the Alphabet, by which the Notes are therein express'd: These Letters being seven, A, B, C, D, E, F, G, I assign them as Names for the seven Musical Notes, taking only the liberty (for better sound-sake, and indication of the Half-Notes places) instead of calling these three Letters, A, E, F, as in the Alphabet, to name them La, Le, fa. When a Flat or Sharp alters the nature of a Note, its Name also admits the like alteration, yet so as to keep the Letter belonging to the Line or Space, thereby making the Change to be no trouble to the Memory, but an help to sing the Notes in Tune. So B being sometimes sharp, and sometimes flat, I call it B when it is sharp, and Be when it is flat, as in [Begin, Before,] with a softer sound, and therefore the more agreeable to a flat or soft Note, as the other is to a sharp. The like is done by C. E being a Vowel, hath

before

The Preface.

before it, when sharp an L, *and when flat an* M. *By this means, we have seven distinct Names for the seven Notes., keeping always the same places in each Cliff, and those Names such as both comply with the* Gam-ut *so much as is need-ful, and also with the Alterations that are made by Flats and Sharps, without burthen to the Memory.*

That there should be seven distinct Names for the seven Notes, is so reasonable, that it is justly to be wondred at, that the Writers of Music should generally assign no more than four *or* six: *This some have complained of, particularly our Learned Dr.* Wallis, *in his Appendix to* Ptolemy's Harmonies, *by him published,* pag. 288. " Sed omnino deest vox septima
" pro sedibus *Ff* voce destitutis; (nam
" quod ibidem habeantur *Fa Ut,* id est,
" alterius syzygiæ:) —— *Quod mirum est*
" *Guidonem non vidisse & præcavisse.* Re-
" centiores aliqui (inter quos Mersen-
" nus) supplent vocem *si* aut huic simi-
" lem.

The next thing, wherein I have endeavoured to facilitate the Learner's Task, is, by shewing a way to Tune the Notes aright in any Octave, *or* Cliff, *without the help of a Master or In-strument:*

The Preface.

strument : To which, I require no more in the *Learner, but that he have either heard, or* can *fing the Notes of* SIX BELLS. *He who hath not Natural Mufic enough to do this, (efpecially in this* Ringing Ifland, *as fome have called it) may be fuppofed not fo defirous of the Art, as to concern himfelf in this or any other method.*

The reafon why I chufe Six Notes, ra-*ther than Five, Eight, or any other Num-ber, is, becaufe the* Half-Note *more naturally and eafily falls in its right place in* Six, *(viz. between the third and fourth Notes) than in any other number of Notes, it being not eafie to fing them falfe, as any one that tryes will find : The reafon is , becaufe if the* Half-Note *be mifplaced, it muft be by Sing-*ing three whole Tones fucceffively, *which is both* unpleafant upon an Inftrument, and difficult to the

* Amiffio autem triplicati Toni, etfi ad perficiendum ubique Diapafon neceffaria, dura tamen fuit canentibus unde ad talem duritiem temperan-dam Artifices divifere tertium illum tonum in femitonia *Ough-predi* Elementa Muficæ inter Opufc. Sect. 25.

* Voice. *As for* Five *Notes or Bells, the Semitone may be ei-ther between the fe-cond and third, or between the third and fourth, and fo can be*

no

The Preface.

no certain guide : And for Eight, they contain two Semitones, and those in no certain
places. Taking therefore Six Notes, or the
Tune of Six Bells, for the Clue to lead the
Learner by, I have applied them to the lea-
ding him through all the places on the Staff
of Lines in each Cliff, both without and with
Flats and Sharps. The conveniency and suffi-
ciency of this Method any one may be satisfied
of, who a little considers it. Notwithstan-
ding that nothing may be wanting that can be
used as an help, I have shewn how to express the Notes upon a Bass-Viol. To these
Directions, they that can procure a Master,
they will be an help both to him and the Learner, in the more speedy and easie attaining
their Ends.

The third thing I have taken in hand, is
reducing the many Cliffs to as few as might
be, or (which is the same) to shew how to
sing true the Notes prick'd in a Cliff one is
a stranger as if they were in another better known. To this purpose, I have made a
Table, by which all the other Cliffs are reduced to the Treble and Bass; so that he who
hath learnt in these only, may be able to sing
his Notes true, tho' prick'd in other Cliffs.
The

The Preface.

The course I take for effecting this, is by the help of the usual Flats and Sharps, to bring the Half-Notes into the same places of a Staff, tho' sign'd with differing Cliffs. By which means, tho' the Notes be sung in another Key, and therefore called by other Names; yet the Semitones being accordingly set in due places by regular Flats or Sharps, the Tune will be truly express'd by the Voice. I know this way is not wholly practicable upon Instruments, especially such as have fixed Stops, which will seem out of Tune when Lessons are played in a wrong Key: But the Voice being at liberty, will naturally rectify those small inequalities of greater and lesser Tones and Semitones, which on an Instrument, being misplac'd, dissatisfy the Ear.

In the Conclusion, For a Praxis, I have added several Psalm Tunes in Three Parts, with Directions how to sing them, to promote that most harmonious and delightful kind of Singing. This requires somewhat more Skill than the Common way, yet is easie enough, at least for a select Company of Persons, with good Voices to attain unto. It would therefore be a commendable thing, if Six, Eight, or more, sober young Men that have good Voices;

The Preface.

Voices, would associate and form themselves into a Quire, seriously and concordantly to sing the Praises of their Creator: A few such in a Congregation (especially if the Clark make one to lead) might in a little time bring into the Church better Singing than is common, and with more variety of good Tunes, as I have known done.

'Tis pity we have not a better Translation of the Singing Psalms publickly in use; however, for Private Families there are several well done, especially the last by Mr. Patrick, which hath met with a general and deserved Esteem. He hath put more of the Psalms into the Metre of the Hundredth, than were in the old Translation, for the sake both of the Measure and Tune, which are both good. This Translation, together with Mr. Barton's Hymns, will abundantly furnish such with apt Matter, whose Piety and Tunable Voices shall dispose them to Psalms and Spiritual Songs. The promoting of this (as to the Tune and Melody) is the chief of my design in this Essay. If therefore any Reader come with no better ends, than to accomplish himself to bear a Part in a Drunken Catch, a Smutty or Atheistical Song, I assure him, there's not a Word here
design'd

The Preface.

design'd for his service, 'till upon better thoughts a Penitential Psalm *should seem more suitable.*

I have only this farther to acquaint the Reader with, That I have not trusted wholly to my own Judgment, (tho' confirm'd by Experiment made) but have communicated these Papers to Persons of Skill and Eminency, whose Approbation hath been my Encouragement to Publish them, with hopes, that they may be serviceable to unprejudic'd Learners.

ERRATA.

Page 27. *in the second and third Lines, instead of* ♭ *read* ♯. Page 48. *line* 13. *for* [*is in time to a Semibreve,*] *should be* [*is equal in time to a Semibreve*] *The word Equal may be added with a Pen at the beginning of the line.* Page 62. *in the first Staff and second Cliff* *there should be another Flat thus* : *Also in the fifth Staff following, the fourth Cliff should have another Flat thus* . Page 66. *under the third Staff, the* (e) *in* Be *may be struck out with a Pen.* Page 89. *last six Notes of the Tune should be thus*

A New

A New and Easie
METHOD
To Learn to
Sing by Book.

CHAP. I.
Of the Scale of Music, and Cliffs.

I Shall not trouble the Practical Reader
with a Mathematical Account of *Inter-*
vals, or how *Eights* are the same, and
how they differ. It will be sufficient
to observe to him, That there are seven Notes
in *Music*, which are commonly expres'd by
these seven Letters of the Alphabet, *A, B, C,*
D, E, F, G; if a Voice or Instrument rise or
fall gradually more than seven Notes, the

B   fol-

following 8*th*, 9*th*, 10*th*, &*c.* will proceed
in the same order, and bear the same relation
each to other as the 1*st*, 2*d*, 3*d*, &*c.* to
which they are respectively Eighths or
Octaves, and that hence every eighth Note
being alike in nature, is called by the same
name with that to which it is an Eighth,
whether above or below it.

That the various Musical Compositions
out of these Notes may (as Languages) be
communicated by Books and Writing, certain *Lines* and *Characters* are devised and
made use of by *Musicians*, of which you have
here an Example.

In this Example (till we come to the Particulars) you may observe these things in
general. First, That the Characters at the
beginning of the Lines are called *Cliffs* or
Keys, opening and signifying what Part or
Pitch of Voice, *viz. Treble, Mean*, or *Bass*,
the Notes properly belong to, and also on
what Line or Space each of the seven Letters
is placed. Secondly, That the five Lines and
Spaces between them serve as Steps whereon
to

to exprefs the degrees of Sound, or Notes afcending and defcending. Thirdly, That the Characters you fee upon the Lines and Spaces ftand for the Notes themfelves, and their different *form* expreffes their *Quantity*, whether longer or fhorter.

Your bufinefs therefore in this and the following Chapters will be, Firft, In the *Gam-ut* to learn the ufe of the *Cliffs*: Secondly, To learn the names of the Lines and Spaces, that you may readily know what to call a Note ftanding upon any of them : Thirdly, To fing thofe Notes in right Tune, both by degrees and leaps : And laftly, How to give each Note its due Quantity of Time.

Having premifed this in general, to give the Learner a profpect of his Task, I fhall proceed to fay fomething of the *Gam-ut* as far as is neceffary to my defign ; which is, That you may underftand thereby the ufe of the *Cliffs*, and the Order and Diftances of the *Notes* as the Parts lye together in a Body.

The

The Gamut or Scale of MUSIC

F	E la	f g / e
D	la sol	d
	C sol fa	c
B	b fa ♯ mi	b
	A la mi re	a
G	sol re ut	g
	F fa ut	F
E	la mi	E / F
	D la sol re	D
C	sol fa ut	C
	B b fa ♯ mi	B
A	la mi re	A / B
	G sol re ut	G
F	fa ut	F / G
	E la mi	E
D	sol re	D / E
	C fa ut	C
B	mi	B / C
	A re	A
Γ	Gammut	G

Treble Part — Middle Part — Base Part

This Scale (consisting of eleven Lines with the intermediate Spaces) contains the places of all the Notes ordinarily made use of in Vocal Music. In the first Column you have the old Names, which I only set down, that you may see what they are. The second Column shews, which of the seven Letters belongs to each Line and Space. The third Column

Column contains the *Cliffs*, or *Signed Keys*, and shews how many Degrees or Notes they are one above the other ; which being known, the other degrees of Distance are easily computed.

Five of these Lines, with their Spaces, are commonly sufficient for the pricking of any Tune , therefore is the *Scale* divided into three Staves or Parts, compassed in by Arched Lines. Of these, the lower Five belong to the *Bass*, and are known to do so by this mark ℈ upon the Line of *F*, commonly called therefore the *F fa ut* Cliff or Key, opening to us what Letters stand upon the other Lines and Spaces, as will be shewn in the next Chapter.

The upper five Lines contain the highest Notes, and belong to the *Treble*, or highest Part: The Key to these Lines is ᵹ, or sometimes *Gs*, on the lower Line save one. The *Tenor* or Middle Part takes in commonly two of the upper or *Treble* Lines, and two of the *Bass* Lines , having one only in the middle proper to its self, on which is set this mark ≣ for the *Cliff*; its proper place is the middle Line, but is oft set on one or other of the other Lines, which ever the *Cliff* stands upon, that Line is the place of *C*,

and

and the other Lines are to be reckoned accordingly. Sometimes also the *Bass* Cliff is removed to the middle Line, and then that Line is *F, &c.* This shifting of the *Cliffs* is troublesom; but general use having made the knowing of them necessary, you must at least *understand* the manner of them.

CHAP. II.

Of the Names of the Lines and Spaces.

HAving shewed you in the *Gamut* how the Notes lye together in a Body, I shall now take them into Parts according to the three *Cliffs,* beginning with the uppermost as most common. And here your first business will be to learn the Names of your *Lines* and *Spaces,* which the *Cliff* or *Key* opens to you.

The Names are seven, express'd in these seven Letters, *A, B, C, D, E, F, G,* which (for better Sound-sake and Reasons hereafter to be given) you must call L*a*, *B*. C*e*, *D,* L*e,* F*â, G,* pronouncing f*â* broad, as in *Fall, Falcon, &c.* These or the like Names are given to the Notes, both because the
Voyce

Voyce is best put forth in expressing some Syllable, and also that the seven Notes might be known by as many distinct Names. Their places in the three *Cliffs* are as in these Examples.

It will be convenient that you begin with and keep to one *Cliff* only at the first, which you please, or which best agrees with your Voice for a pitch high or low; when you have gone through all the Rules, and are perfect in that, you may proceed to the other.

You need not trouble your self with the *Tenor* or *C* Cliff, which keeps no certain place; the ninth Chapter shews you how to sing any thing you meet with prick'd in that Cliff.

Before you proceed any farther, you must be ready at naming your Lines and Spaces, so as to tell readily, as soon as you cast your Eye upon any Line or Space, what Letter it is called by. The *Cliff* leads you to all the rest, for beginning thereat, and ascending, the Letters lye in order; and descending, you name them backward.

The Dash-lines that you see above and below are only added, when the Notes ascend above, or descend below the Staff.

CHAP. III.

Of the distances Note from Note, as to Sound.

THE distances of Notes one from another, as to sound, are not all equal, but
in

in the rising or falling of any eight Notes,
there be two lesser distances called *Semitones*
or Half Notes, which must be well known
by their places in the Staff of Lines.

The better to remember them, take the
Rules in these Rhimes.

In ev'ry Octave half Notes two
There are, the which their Places shew;
One half Note is from B to Ce,
The other lies 'twixt Fa and Le.

This Rule shews the ordinary places
where the half Notes are to be sung, when
there be no *Flats* or *Sharps* set on the Lines,
to wit, between B and Ce, and between
Le and Fa.

What is to be done when you have these
marks (♭) and (✳) upon the Lines, shall be
shewed in *Chap. 6.*

In these Staves you have the Notes gradually ascending, of which those Pairs marked with Arches are distant half a Note.

This

G.
F.
E.
D.
C.
B.
A.
G.

1
2
3
4
5
6

This Figure reprefents to the Eye the diftances of the feven Notes one from another, the Letters guiding you to the Particulars; where, as you fee B Ce, and Le ʃá, lying nearer than the reſt, fo are their founds to be nearer.

That you may with your own Voice exprefs, and thereupon obferve the difference between whole and half Note diftances, fing thefe fix words, *One, two, three four, five, fix,* diftinctly in the Tune of *Six Bells,* and after you have done fo feveral times fing only 1, 2, 3, 4, and ftop there, repeating 3, 4, by themfelves for they are diftant in found a *Semitone,* all the reſt are a *Tone* or *whole Note* diftant each from the next. By a little obfervation you will perceive the 3 and 4 Bells or Notes to be lefs diftant in found than the other.

The Numbers 1, 2, 3, 4, 5, 6, in the former Figure, ſhew to the Eye the feveral diftances of the fix Notes, where Le is the firſt, D the fecond, &c. and the third and fourth are Ce, B, diftant half a Note or Tone.

CHAP.

CHAP. IV.

Of Tuning the Notes.

Sect. I. THe readieft way to learn to tune your Notes aright, is by following either the Voice of one skill'd in *Mufic*, or fome tuned Inftrument that hath Frets or Keys, which are the only ways hitherto made ufe of, that of a Mafter being moft common; but becaufe (in the Country efpecially) oft-times none of thefe can be had, the following Directions are laid down, which may fuffice for one that hath a Mufical Ear. The only poftulate is, That the Learner hath ever heard, or can fing, the Notes of *Six Bells*, which Requifite I think few are without, whofe Genius inclines them to *Mufic*.

Suppofing therefore that you can fing 1, 2, 3, 4, 5, 6, right, I fhall proceed by the help of thofe Notes, to lead you to all the reft.

Obferve, That when you begin to fing the firft Note, on what Line or Space foever it ftand, you may fing it with what Tone you pleafe, high or low, (as to the pitch of your Voice)

Voice) with this Caution, That you count
how many Notes you have above or below
it, that the pitch of your Voice may be so as
to reach both, without squeeking or grumbling. After you have tuned the first, or
any one Note, all the rest follow necessarily
in their due distances above and below it.

Example I. For applying of the Six Notes.

Begin with the first Bar, and with your
Voice high, sing the six Notes you see on the
Staff several times, calling them by the
Numbers over, *viz.* 1, 2, 3, 4, 5, 6, as you
did in the former Chapter; which when
you have done, sing the same Notes, calling
them by their Names, La, So, Fa, La, Sol, Fa,
in the Tune of *Six Bells.*

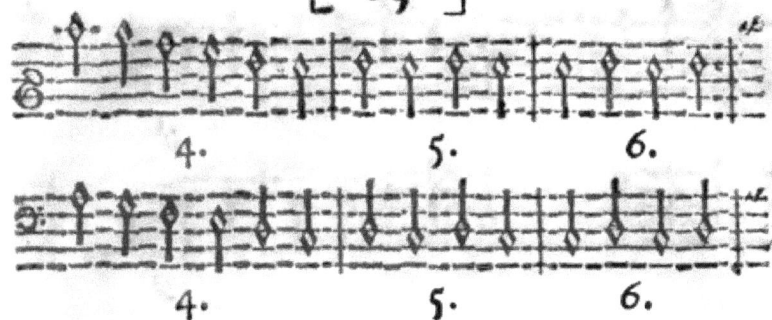

4.   5.   6.

4.   5.   6.

2. In the second and third Bars sing the
two first Notes of the *six* by themselves,
both forward and backward.   In the fourth
Bar repeat all *six*, and in the fifth and sixth
Bars repeat the two last Notes, D, Ce, both
forward and backward.   These Notes are
distant a whole Tone, which distance, by
often repeating these Notes in the second,
third, fourth, fifth, and sixth Bars, you
will the better know and distinguish from
lesser.

7.

7.

In the seventh Bar, after all *six*, repeat the
three last often over, first down, LE, D, Ce;
LE, D, Ce. &c. and then backward, Ce, D,
LE; Ce, D, LE, &c.   In

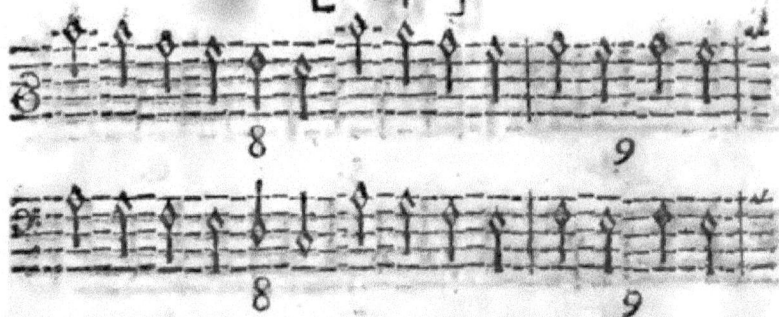

In the eighth Bar, after all *six*, repeat often the four first, LA, ☉, FÂ, LE; and in singing them, obferve efpecially the two Notes Fâ, LE, becaufe their diftance is a *Semitone*; therefore afterwards in the ninth Bar, fing them by themfelves fo often, 'till you have fix'd in your fancy their diftance, for this you will find the hardeft thing, to fing true the *half Notes* in their places.

In the tenth Bar, fing the four firft Notes both down and up.

In the Eleventh Bar, firft fing the fix Notes in order, then repeat the four laft, Fâ, LE,

D,

D, Ce, leaving out the two first Notes, Lа,
G, and still marking the *Semitone* between
ƒâ, Lе, which two Notes sing by themselves in the twelfth Bar.

In the thirteenth Bar sing ƒâ, Lе, D, Ce,
down and up as they are prick'd, and observe the three last, ƒâ, Lе, ƒâ, because it
is a common Close, or ending of Tunes.

Note: If any where you doubt whether
you sing right a repeated part of the *Six
Notes*, (as here in the 11*th* and 13*th* Bars)
sing over again all six in order, and then try
at the Parts by themselves.

Example

Example II.

Sect. II. Having often gone over the former Examples, you may now proceed by the same Clue of the *Six Notes* to descend three Steps lower, *viz.* to ⑤, which is an *Octave* to the second Note of the first *Six*.

1. In the first Bar begin with a high pitch of your Voice, and having sung (as in the former Examples) L𝔄, ⑤, 𝔉𝔞̃, L𝔈, 𝔇, ℭe, leave out L𝔄, and sing only the five last; then in the second Bar repeat only the three last, L𝔈, 𝔇, ℭe, but call them not now L𝔈, 𝔇, ℭe, but *One, two, three,* altering the Names, but not the Tune. This

This done, in the third Bar fing the *Six Notes* from L℧ to ℧, calling them as Bells, *One, two, three, four, five, fix*; fo that your three firft of thefe, be the fame in Tune with the three laft of the former *Six* : After you have fung them as Bells, 1, 2, 3, 4, 5, 6, four or five times, fing them again as oft, calling them by their Names, L℧, D, ℭe, ℬ, L℧, ℧.

In the fourth Bar fing the four firft, L℧, D, ℭe, ℬ, three or four times, and then repeat ℭe, ℬ, by themfelves, obferving well their diftance or difference, which is a *Semitone*, like to ƒâ, L℧, above.

In the fifth Bar, after you have fung all fix, repeat the four laft, ℭe, ℬ, L℧, ℧, often over, keeping them in the fame Tune that they had in all fix; fo fhall ℭe, ℬ, be diftant half a Note : Then fing them backward, ℧, L℧, ℬ, ℭe, repeating ℬ, ℭe, at the end, as you did L℧, ƒâ, in the 13*th* Bar before.

C

In

In the sixth Bar, after you have sung all
six in order, sing the three first, LE, D, Ce,
and stop there ; then sing those three over
again in the same Tune, calling them not
LE, D, Ce, but, *Three, four, five,* several
times : Then proceed to the seventh Bar,
and adding two Notes above, sing them
as five Bells, *One, two, three, four, five,*
three or four times, and then call them by
their Names, G, Fâ, LE, D, Ce. This
done, proceed to the eighth Bar, and to the
other five, add B, LA, G, to make up an
Octave,

Octave, remembering the Diftances as you fung them in the former Examples; fo have you now a whole *Octave*, or eight *Notes* from ☉ to ☉, which you muſt practice both down and up; and when you are perfect in it, fo as to fing your Diftances true, with the *Semitones* in their right places, the following Directions will lead you through the reft of the Notes to fing any other *Octave*, beginning at any other Letter.

In the ninth Bar begin at L☰ again, and begin the fix Notes, L☰, D, ☰e, B, L☰, ☉. in order; which done, repeat the two laſt Notes, L☰, ☉, by themſelves: Then proceed to the tenth Bar, and fing theſe fix, L☰, ☉, ſa, L☰, D, ☰e, fo that L☰ and ☉ be the fame in Tune as they were in the former fix.

If your Voice will not reach to ☰e at the pitch you began the firſt Bar, fing as far as you can, or begin L☰ in the ninth Bar higher, finging theſe three laſt Bars diſtinct from the foregoing.

 In

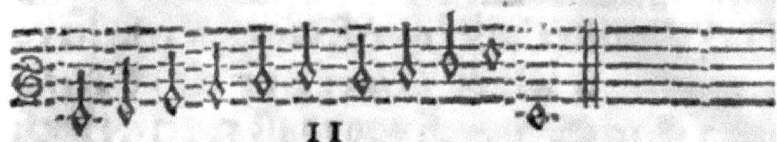

11

In the eleventh Bar fing your laft fix Notes backward, Ce, D, LC, fâ, S, LA, rifing from Ce to LA; then going one Step backward to S, rife to Ce, (as in the fifth Bar before) which is an *Octave* or *Eighth* to the lower Ce.

I have omitted thefe three laft Bars in the *Bafs* Cliff, becaufe the Notes would run too far below the five Lines.

Thus are you gone through all the Notes upon the five Lines and their Spaces, with the half Notes in their own places; in pra-ctifing upon which, make not too much haft, but by often Repetitions fix in your fancy the diftances Note from Note.

CHAP.

CHAP. V.
Of Rising and Falling by Leaps.

YOur former rising and falling was by *Degrees* or *Steps* of *whole* and *half Notes*, your next business is to learn to rise and fall your Voice by *Leaps* of *Thirds*, *Fourths*, *Fifths*, *Sixths*, and *Eighths*, that is, by skipping over one, two, three, or more Notes.

Having begun with *falling* the *Six Notes* by Steps, I shall proceed the same way in setting down the *Leaps*.

Note: That in singing these following Examples, it will be convenient in the passage by degrees, to give those Notes a longer time of prolation, which are to be repeated in the *Leap*, that their Tune by themselves may the better be remembred: Therefore have I in the Examples pricked the Notes of the *Leap* in *Semibreves*, which are longer Notes than the other with Tails, called *Minims*.

Begin

Begin with the first Bar; where, having
fung the *fix Notes* once or twice, begin them
in the fecond Bar, and ftop at the third Note,
finging only LE, D, Ce; after which, it
will be eafie to skip over D, and fing LE,
Ce, which diftance, being two whole Tones,
is called a *Greater Third*.

In the third Bar, you may firft fing over
the *fix Notes*, as in the firft, and then fing
only thefe four, LE, D, Ce, B, ftopping
at B; this done, fing LE, B, omitting D
and Ce: But that you may be fure you tune
them aright, go often over all *fix*, and then
the

the four firſt by degrees, immediately before you try the *Leap*.

In like manner you muſt do by the other Bars.

In the fourth Bar you leap from L℃ to LℭI, which being a prefect Concord, called a *Fifth*, is the oftner to be repeated. You may eaſily know this *Leap*, if you take notice, That it is always from any Line or Space, to the next Line or Space ſave one; as you may ſee in the the fourth Bars of the two *Cliffs*.

6.   7.

8.

9.

10.

Theſe

6.   7.

8.

9.

10.

These four laſt Bars lead you to riſe the ſame Diſtances or Leaps that you fell before. In the *Treble Cliff*, I have repeated the *ſix Notes*, every Bar with ſo many both *falling* and *riſing* as contain the *Leap*. In the other *Cliff* I have omitted ſo doing for brevity. You may ſee by the *Treble Cliff* how to proceed in the reſt.

In General, To riſe or fall by *Leaps*, firſt proceed *ſtep by ſtep*, from the one Note to the other, and then paſs over the intermediate Note or Notes; as you ſee done in the Examples.

There

There is yet remaining to be fung an *Octave*, (the chief Concord) for which, look back to the fixth, feventh, and eighth Bars of the fecond Example of the laft Chapter, and the Directions belonging to thim, by which, having fung *eight Notes* in order, falling by degrees, it will be eafie to leap from the firft to the eighth, and from the eighth to the firft, as here.

In the thirteenth Bar, fing eight Notes, beginning a C e above, (to which you may proceed in the manner you did to the other eight, from G to G,) and then rife and fall the *Octaves.* The like may be done in other Octaves.

Sect. II. Of thefe *Leaps,* a *Fourth, Fifth,* and *Eighth,* keep always the fame Diftances in all places; fo that all *Fourths* are alike in Tune; in like manner, all *Fifths,* and all *Eighths*; but as to *Thirds* and *Sixths,* they have

have a *Greater* and *Leſſer*; *viz.* a *Greater*
and *Leſſer Third*, and a *Greater* and *Leſſer
Sixth*; as will appear in the following Examples.

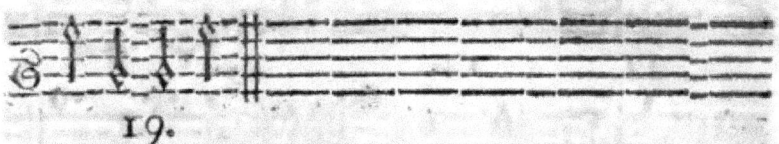

14.   15.   16.

17.   18.

19.

In the fourteenth Bar, you leap firſt from
𝕲 to 𝕯, which is a *Fourth*, whoſe diſtance
is two *Tones* and an half; *viz.* from 𝕲 to
𝕱á, and from L𝕰 to 𝕯, are each a *Tone*;
and from 𝕱â to L𝕰 a *Semitone*. In like
manner in the fifteenth Bar, from 𝕱â to ℭe
is a *Fourth*, of equal diſtance with the other;
for from 𝕱â to L𝕰 is a *Semitone*; and from
L𝕰 to 𝕯, and from 𝕯 to ℭe, are two *Tones*
more; and ſo will you find the *Fifths* and
Eighths to have the ſame diſtances, though
in different places, if you reckon the intermediate Diſtances.

Is

In the end of the sixteenth Bar, you have a greater *Third* from D to G, rising and falling. These Notes D and G, are distant two whole Tones.

In the seventeenth Bar you have a lesser *Third*, *viz.* from Ce to LA, they being distant but a *Tone* and a half.

In the eighteenth Bar you have a lesser *Sixth*, from G above to B, they being distant three *Tones*, and two *Semitones*, or (which is all one) a *Fourth*, and a lesser *Third*.

In the nineteenth Bar you have a greater *Sixth*, from LE to G below, which are distant four *Tones* and an half; all which you may easily count, and see represented to the Eye in the *Scales* in the sixth Chapter.

Of these Distances, an *Eighth* and *Fifth* are called *Perfect Cords*, two Notes being distant an *Eighth* or *Fifth*, and sung or play'd together, yielding a most pleasing Harmony to the Ear. A *Third* and *Sixth* are called *Imperfect Cords*, or less pleasing; the other Distances are *Discords*, of a harsh and unpleasant sound.

CHAP. VI.

Of Flats and Sharps.

Sect. I. IN the former Examples the two *Semitones*, or *Half-Note Distances*, were in their proper places, *viz.* between ♩, ℭe, and Lℭ, ƒâ; which places they do not always keep, but are shifted variously, sometimes one, and sometimes both. When the *Semitones* are thus shifted, is known by these marks (♭) and (※), called a *Flat* and a *Sharp*, or (as in the Latin) a *Hard* and *Soft*.

When you see this mark (♭) set upon Line or Space at the beginning of the Staff, it denotes, that all the Notes upon that Line or Space through the whole Song, are to be sung half a Note lower than otherwise they should have been : But if in the middle of a Tune it be set before some one Note, it only flattens that Note.

There be two places where *Flats* are commonly set, *viz.* ♩ and Lℭ ; and then ♩

is brought nearer to 𝕬, and L𝕰 to 𝕯. In this cafe, that there may be a correfpondency between the Names and the Notes, and thereby the Names be a help to the right tuning of them, I have affigned two different Names to each, yet fo, that the Letter it felf is not changed; and therefore the Names of the Lines and Spaces, both *Flat* and *Sharp*, are eafily remembred, without the trouble that arifes from the confufed fhifting of *Sol*, *La*, *Mi*, *Fa*, in the old way.

The difference you are to make, is this: That when 𝕭 hath no *Flat* upon it, you call it 𝕭, as you do in the Alphabet; but when it is *Flat*, call it 𝕭e, as in *Before*, *Belong*, &c. which is a flatter or fofter found, and fuits the better with a flat Note.

So for 𝕰, when it hath no *Flat* upon it, call it L𝕰; and when it hath, call it M𝕰; fo is the Letter 𝕰 preferved in both. You may remember them by this Rhime:

When 𝕭 *is Flat, you call it* 𝕭e;
When L𝕰 *is Flat, then call it* M𝕰.

The

The (⁂) *Sharp* is of a contrary nature to the *Flat*, and makes the Notes before which it is set, a Semitone higher than their own diſtance; and that through the whole Tune, if it be ſet at the beginning of the Lines; or only one Note, if ſet before it in the middle.

There are two places where *Sharps* are uſually ſet, *viz.* ꟻ and ℭ, which being of their own nature *flat* Notes, are hereby made *ſharp*, or a whole ſone diſtant from the next below them.

In this caſe, for diſtinction, when ꟻ hath no *ſharp* upon it, call it ꟻâ, (as hitherto you have done) ſounding (â) broad and ſoft, which beſt agrees with a *flat* Note; but when it is a *ſharp*, call it ꟻa, with a ſharper ſound of (a) as in *Famous, Favour*: Likewiſe when ℭ hath no *ſharp*, call it ℭe, as in the firſt Syllable of *Ceſar*; but when it is *ſharp*, call it ℭ, as in the Alphabet, which is a ſharper Sound, and ſo is the fitter Name.

When ℭe *is ſharp. then call it* ℭ;
When ꟻâ *is ſharp, then* ꟻa *'t muſt be.*

Here

Here let not the Learner think he hath met with any great difficulty by this alteration of Diſtances, for ſtill there will be but two half Notes in every *Octave*, though in other places ; and theſe their Names will mind you to ſing *flat* or *ſharp*.

For the better remembrance of the *Semitones* places , take this Rule :

Under each (♭) Flat *an half Note lies,*
But o're a (✳) Sharp *the half doth riſe.*

That is, when this mark (♭) is ſet upon a Line or Space, it is but half a Note to the next degree below ; and when this mark (✳) is ſet upon a Line or Space, it is half a Note to the next degree above.

That what hath been hitherto ſaid of the Places of whole and half Notes, with their alteration by *Flats* and *Sharps*, may the better be conceived in order to Practice, I have inſerted a Figure in the following Page, which repreſents them to the Eye in two *Octaves*, beginning below at 𝔊.

Five

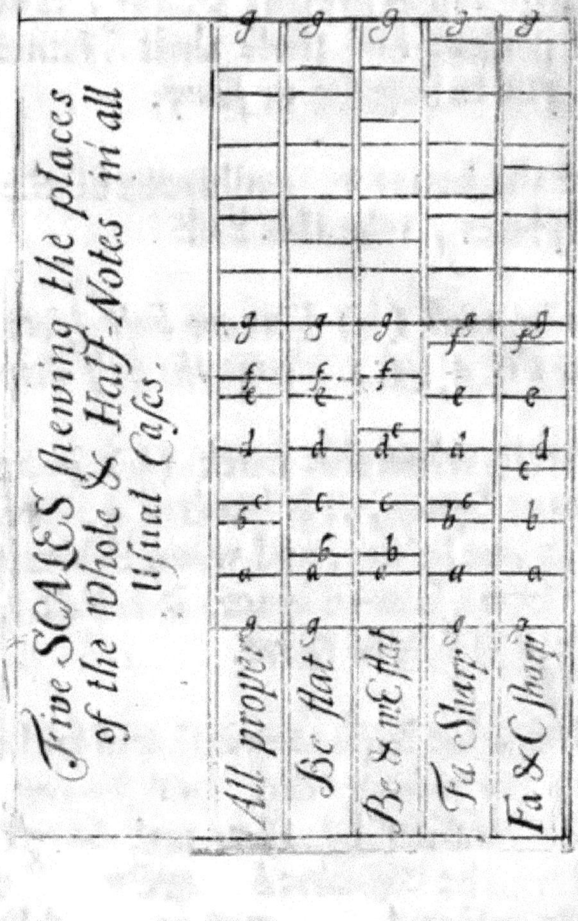

Five SCALES shewing the places of the Whole & Half-Notes in all Usual Cases.

All proper

Be Flat

Be & mE flat

Fa Sharp

Fa & C Sharp

This Figure confifts of Five *Scales* : In the firft, are all the *Notes* in their proper Order and Diftances.

In

In the second Scale, 𝕭 is *flat*, that is, half a Note nearer to 𝕬; the reſt keeping their places.

In the third Scale, 𝕭 and 𝕰 are *flat*, and ſo the two half Notes are between 𝕬, 𝕭, and 𝕯, 𝕰.

In the fourth Scale, 𝕱 is *ſharp*, that is, raiſed half a Note nearer to 𝕲; the reſt keeping their proper places as in the firſt.

In the fifth Scale, 𝕱 and 𝕮 are both *ſharp*, and ſo the two Semitones are between 𝕮, 𝕯, and 𝕱, 𝕲.

In all which you may ſee, that ſtill there be two *Half-Note Diſtances*, neither more nor fewer in every *Octave*. 𝕲, 𝕬, and 𝕯, keep their places, having ſeldom either *Flats* or *Sharps* on them, except in one ſingle Note, or two ſometimes in a Tune.

Note: That when a *Flat* or *Sharp* is ſet at the beginning of the Staff, the *Octaves* or *Eighths* muſt be marked with the ſame, as you will ſee in the Examples following.

D   Sect.

Sect. II. Having ſhewed you the nature of
Flats and *Sharps*, I ſhall now proceed to apply the *ſix Notes* to the Staff of Lines, and
firſt with Ee Flat.

I.   2.   3.

4.   5.

I.   2.   3.

4.   5.

In the three firſt Bars, you have the *ſix
Notes* thrice repeated, in ſuch manner, as
to paſs through the whole **Staff**, and lead
you to tune all the Diſtances aright. In
ſinging theſe Examples, begin with your
Voice at as high a pitch as you can well
reach; and having ſung the firſt Bar as in
the former Chapter, proceed to the *ſix Notes*

12

in the ſecond Bar, of which, the two firſt
D, Ce, muſt be as in Name, ſo in Tune, the
ſame with the two laſt Notes of the former
ſix.

Repeat this ſecond Bar often, that you
may know how to ſing Be *flat*, which now
you muſt call ſo, and not B.

In the third Bar, repeat La, G, Fâ, and
make them up *ſix*, by ſinging down to Ce,
(if your Voice will reach ſo far.)

In the fourth Bar, begin the *ſix Notes*
at D, and ſing them down and up.

Then in the fifth Bar, ſing the five firſt
down and up, ſtill keeping the Semitone between Be and La.

By theſe two laſt Bars, you learn to riſe
from Fâ and G with Be *flat*, which are two
uſual Keys.

6.   7.

8.   9.

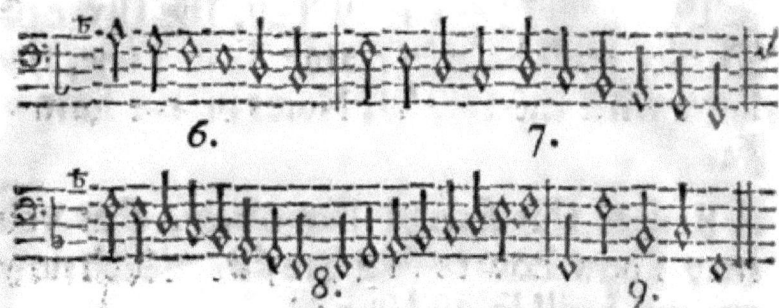

6.   7.

8.   9.

In the sixth Bar, sing the *six Notes*, beginning at La; then in the seventh Bar repeat the four last, Fa, Le, D, Ce, and going one step backward to D, sing on the *six Notes* down to Fa; from thence, rise an Eighth to Fa, in the eighth Bar, where it will be easie, after two or three times singing over the foregoing Notes, to sing the whole *Octave* orderly, both down and up.

Note: That this *Octave*, of Fa with Be flat, is the same in Tune with that of Ce, in the last Bar of *Chap.* 4. wherein the eight Notes lye in the most natural and tuneable order. At the end are added *Leaps*, which first you may pace by Degrees or Steps, and then leap.

S. ā.

Sect. III. When ℬ and 𝔈 are both made
flat by this mark (♭) , then will your *six
Notes* lye as in thefe Examples.

In the firft three Bars, you have the *six
Notes* in their feveral places with ℬe and
M𝔈 *flat*; in finging of which, follow the
Directions given in the end of the laft Se-
ction, efpecially noting M𝔈 and ℬe, which
are the *flat* Notes; therefore in the fourth
Bar, after all *six*, repeat the four laft from
M𝔈 to ℬe down and up, as they are prick'd.

Note: That the firft *six Notes* begin moft
conveniently at 𝔇 above, in the *Bafs* Cliff.

Sect. IV. Fa (⁂) Sharp.

When you see a (⁂) *Sharp* at the beginning of any Line or Space, it denotes, that all the Notes thereon, must be sung half a Note higher than their ordinary place, as is before said; when *fa* is therefore to be sung *sharp*, the *six Notes* lye as in these Examples.

In

In the first three Bars, you have the *fix*
Notes in their feveral places, as they lye
when ꜰa is *fharp*. Begin them with your
Voice as high as you can, and defcend in
the method as is before directed, efpecially
marking ꜰa the *fharp Note*, which now you
muft call fo, and not ꜰá, broad, as before.

In the fourth Bar, you have the method
ufed in *Sect*.2, to lead you through the *Octave*
from ♉ to ♋, which is *in Tune* the fame
with that there, from ꜰá to ꜰá, with ♌e
flat; and in *Chap*. 4. from ♋e to ♋e.

Sect. V. ꜰa *and* ♋ (✳) *Sharp.*

When ꜰa and ♋ are both *fharp*, the two
Semitones are removed a degree higher, fo
that now they lye between ♋, ♌, and ꜰa,♋;
in this cafe the *fix Notes* lye as in thefe Examples.

I need

[40]

I need add no more Directions; what is said in the other cases being sufficient. Sing the Notes as you see them prick'd.

The changing of the Names, Ce and ſâ, into C and ſa, will, when you come to those Notes, mind you of singing them *ſharp*.

If at any time you meet with two Notes together, upon the same Line or Space, whereof one is *flat*, and the other *ſharp*, you will find it a little difficult at first to alter your Voice from *Flat* to *Sharp*, or the contrary, in one and the same Note: If you therefore obſerve the method of the following Examples, it will be ſome help to you.

Example 1.

Suppoſe you were to ſing the Notes of the firſt Bar, where C *ſharp* follows Ce *flat*: In this caſe, firſt ſkip the ſharp Note, and ſing

fing the next above it, *viz.* D, as in the
fecond Bar; and from thence, fall half a
Note to the *Sharp* C under, as if you were
going to make a *Clofe*, like as in the 13*th*
Bar of *Chap. IV. Sect.* 1. Sing the Notes
in the fecond Bar feveral times; by which
means, you will at laft perceive the difference between C e *flat*, and C *fharp*, and fo
may you go back, and fing the Notes of the
firft Bar.

Example 2.

In the firft
Bar of the fe-
cond Example

1.   2.

you have fa, firft with a (✵) before it, and
then fâ proper, without. That you may
fing them true, firft fing the Notes in the
fecond Bar, G, fa; G, fâ; (which you
are fuppofed able to do by the foregoing
Directions:) And in finging, take notice
of the difference between the firft fa *fharp*,
and the fecond fâ *flat*; which when you
have done, you will the eafier fing the firft
Bar.

And thus have we gone through all the
ufual Varieties of the *Tones* and *Semitones*
placcs.

places. To him that is perfect in these, an odd irregular *Flat* or *Sharp* now and then will not break square.

I have been the larger in these three last Chapters, that I might make all as plain as might be to the meanest Capacity. They who need not so much, may the sooner pass it over.

That you may the better know where to begin your *Six Notes* in all cases, these Five *Rules* following are easily committed to memory.

I.

All Pro-per. { *When there's no* Flat *nor* Sharp, *you may Begin your* Six *at* L𝕮 *and* L𝕬 :

II.

Be flat. { *But When a* Flat *is set on* 𝕭 , *Begin the* Six *at* L𝕬 *and* 𝕯.

III.

𝕭e *and* M𝕮 flat { *When* Flats *at* 𝕭e *and* M𝕮 *are fixt. From* 𝕲 *and* 𝕯 *descend your* Six.

IV.

ꟻa sharp. { *If* ꟻa *alone be* Sharp, *begin From* 𝕭 *and* L𝕮 *your Notes to sing.*

V.

ꟻa *and* 𝕮 sharp. { *If* Sharps *both* ꟻa *and* 𝕮, *affect Where to begin* ꟻa, 𝕭 *direct.*

CHAP.

CHAP. VII.

*Shewing how to expreſs the Notes on a
Baſs-Viol for guiding of the Voice.*

THo' to an ordinary Capacity the former
Directions may ſuffice; yet for the
ſake of ſuch as may have the conveniency
of an Inſtrument to help them, I have added
this Chapter.

First, it will be convenient, that upon the
Neck of the *Viol*, at each Fret or Stop, you
put a Letter with a Pen or Pencil, to diſtin-
guiſh them by. Begin at the end of the
Strings next to the Pegs, and there put *(a)*;
at the firſt Fret next to that, put *(b)*; at the
ſecond Fret, put *(c)*; and ſo on, to the 7*th*
Fret, which muſt have *(h)*.

Having thus done, tune the fifth String
(or biggeſt ſave one) to a convenient pitch
for a low Note; then wind up the fourth
String 'till it be *Uniſon*, or the ſame ſound
with the fifth String ſtop'd with your Finger
on *(h)* Fret; ſo will theſe two Strings be in
Tune for the expreſſing of eight Notes.

The

The Strings being in Tune, fit down and place the *Viol* between your Legs, and resting the Neck upon your left hand, draw the Bow so upon the fifth String unstop'd, as to give a clear sound, to which, tune your Voice, pronouncing the Note ☉ : Then stop the fifth String upon the Fret *(c)* with a Finger of your left Hand, and drawing the Bow upon the same String, tune your Voice thereto, expressing La a whole Tone distant from ☉.

In like manner proceed to stop the fifth String at *(e)* and *(f)* ; then drawing the Bow over the fourth String, first unstop'd or open, then stop'd at *(c)*, *(d)*, and *(f)*, one after another, and tune your Voice to the Notes respectively, calling them in order from ☉, La, B, Ce, D, Le, Fa, ☉, as you see in the first Example, where you have the Notes rising and falling on the five Lines; and underneath, two Lines representing the fourth and fifth Strings of the Viol, on which are the Letters, shewing where to stop the several Notes.

In the second Example, you have an *Octave* ascending and descending with Be and Me *flat*, by which (compared with the first Example) you may learn how to sing any
other

other Note *flat* or *sharp:* You may see also, that two Frets or Stops make a whole Note, or Tone; and one Fret, an half Note, or Semitone.

The third Example shews you how to express 𝕱 a *sharp*, and 𝕮 both *flat* and *sharp*.

All Proper.

Example 1.

Fourth String.
Fifth String.

𝕭 *and* 𝕰 *Flat.*

Example 2.

Fourth String.
Fifth String.

𝕱 a *sharp.*   𝕮 *sharp.*

Exam. 3.

Fourth String.
Fifth String.

CHAP.

CHAP. VIII.

Of Time, or the Quantity of Notes.

BEfides the giving to *Notes* their right Tune or Sound, there muft be a due obfervation of the Quantity of each *Note*, as to its *Time* of Prolation.

The diverfity of Notes, according to their diftance or difference in Tune, is before treated of, and is known by the feveral Lines and Spaces on which they ftand. Their difference in *Time* is known by diverfity of Figure.

The Names and Figures of the ufual *Notes*, in refpect of *Time*, and their *Refts*, are as follows.

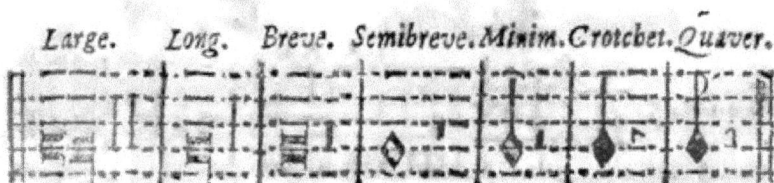

Large.   Long.   Breve.   Semibreve. Minim. Crotchet. Quaver.

The Strokes or Marks you fee after each Note, are called *Paufes*, or *Refts*; and they denote a ceafing or intermiffion of Sound
for

for the Time of the Notes they are joyned to.

Their Proportion to each other, you have in the following Scheme.

For Common Time.

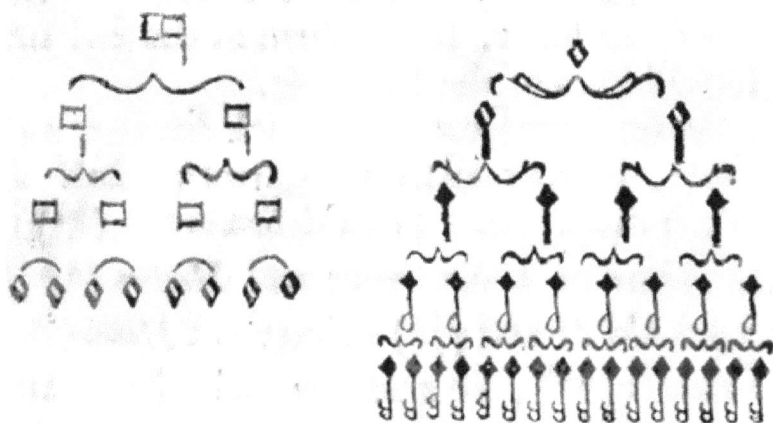

For Tripla Time.

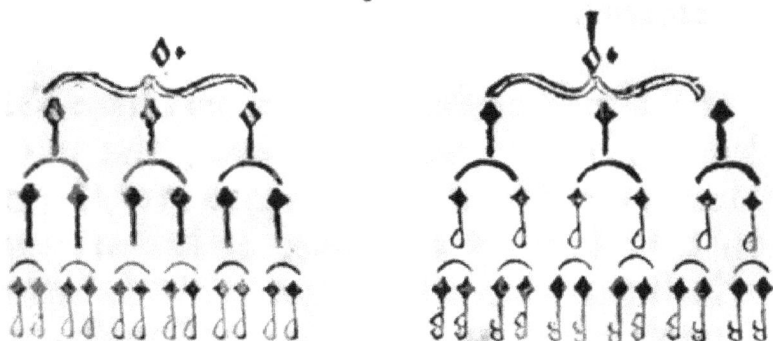

One

One *Large* (▭) is equal in Time to two (▯) *Longs*; one (▯) *Long*, to two (▫) *Breves*; one (▫) *Breve*, to two (○) *Semibreves*; and so on, each Longer being equal in Time to two of the Shorter. Of these, the *Large* and *Long* are now of no other use, than to shew the Time of the *Paufes* or *Rests*, set by them in the first and second Bars of the Example.

When you see a (.) Prick set after any Note, it encreaseth its Quantity half as much more: So a prick'd *Semibreve* (○•) is in Time to a *Semibreve* and *Minim* (○♩); a prick'd *Minim* (♩•) as long as a *Minim* and *Crotchet* (♩♩), or a *Minim* and a half; and a prick'd *Crotchet* (♩•) as much as a *Crotchet* and *Quaver* (♩♩). You will have Examples afterward.

By the foregoing Scheme, you have the Proportion of Note to Note; the next thing is to know, how to give every Note its true Time in any Song or Lesson; for which purpose, every Tune is divided into Parcels, called *Times*, by Lines or Bars struck across the Staff.

In

In singing, or playing upon an Instrument, the due Quantity of Time from *Bar* to *Bar*, is kept by an even Motion of the Hand or Foot, up and down.

This Motion of the Hand, for keeping of *Time*, is sometimes slower, and sometimes quicker, according as the Air of the Tune is grave or light; therefore are there two usual sorts of Time.

I. *Common Time*, marked thus ₵ at the beginning of the Tune, in which, every Bar contains a *Semibreve* (◯) in Time, which you may value, by counting, *One*, *two*, *three*, *four*, in an ordinary reading time, for its length; of which, count 1, 2, with your Hand up, and 3, 4, with it down. By pra-ctising thus your Hand, you will get a habit of keeping due time.

Example.

In this Example, you have two Staves of
Lines; in the upper are *Semibreves*, each of
which is a Time, and fills up a Bar: In the
lower Staff, you have under each *Semibreve*
four *Crotchets*, being, together, equal in Time
to a *Semibreve*. Between the Staves, you
have

gures, 1, 2, 3, 4, in each Bar,
re to pronounce in Tune with
for the gaging the motion of
p and down.
k C for *Common Time* be rever-
it denotes, that you muſt double
of the ordinary Time.

t *Time*, marked thus C3, is
lotes have a light and ſwifter
n *Jiggs*, and Airy *Songs*. In
the Notes go by Threes, and
es three, ſometimes ſix *Crotchets*
or Bar; the Time-Note there-
e *Crotchets* in a Bar, is ⟨, and
ets to a Bar, ⟨; which latter,
venient for the motion of the
at three *Crotchets* may be ſung
id up, and three with it down;
ly be done with *Minims* when
ith three of them, or equiva-
ar; *viz.* making two Bars as
ree *Minims* (or one Bar) with
, and three with it down.
ne *Minims* in this kind of *Tripla*,
ity about the length of *Crotchets*
ime.

An

*An Example of Six Crotchets to a Bar,
out of Mr. Simpson's Compendium.*

Example I.

Example II.

Sometimes the longer Notes (as the *Minims* in the first Example) are prick'd black,
and without Tayls, thus (♦), and then the
two first Bars will be prick'd as in the second
Example.

Ano-

Another Example of Tripla Time, *which being a Tune commonly known, may possibly the better hint the Time and Humour of it to the Reader.*

The Flatteries of Fate.

Besides the Notes themselves, and the marks for their Rests, as before, you will sometimes meet with these following Marks.

1. First, a *Directer*, thus (✓), which is set at the end of the Staff of Lines, to shew readily where to go on at the beginning of the next Staff, as in the last Example.

2. A *Tye*, thus ⌒, over two or more Notes, ſignifying that they muſt be ſung to one Syllable, or ſtruck with one motion of the Bow upon an Inſtrument.

3. A Note of *Repetition* (𝄋): This ſet over a Note, ſhews, that from thence you muſt repeat the following over again.

4. A *Hold* (𝄐), which ſet over any Note, ſhews, that it muſt be held to a longer Time than is expreſt by the Note it ſelf.

5. A *Double Bar* 𝄁: This is ſet at a *Cloſe*, or End of a Strain. If it be prick'd thus 𝄇, it ſignifies, that the foregoing Strain muſt be repeated.

6. When you ſee an *Arch* or *Crooked Line* ſtruck over two Notes that have a Bar between them, it ſignifies, that thoſe two Notes are to be ſung or play'd but as one, equal in Time to both; which happens, when the Bar for dividing of Time falls out in the middle of ſome long Note, as in this Example following.

The

The two *Crotchets* with the ftroke over them, are to be fung as one *Minim*, the Hand or Foot ftriking Time in the middle of it.

More Examples to exercife the Voice in rifing and falling Thirds, Fourths, and Fifths, in Notes of differing Meafures.

Thirds falling.

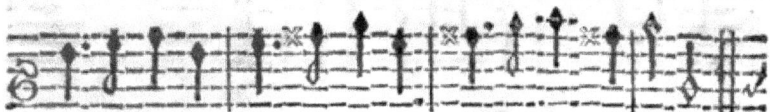

Thirds rifing.

E 4

Fourths.

Fourths.

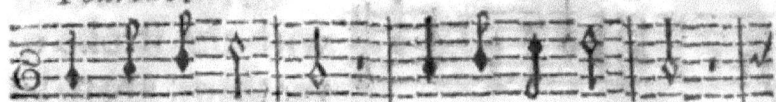

Fifths.

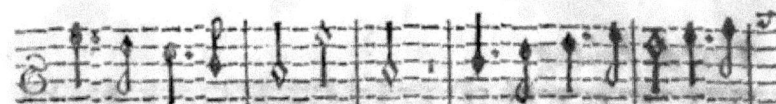

If you obferve the Quantities of the Notes in thefe Examples, you will find each Bar to contain fuch Notes, whofe Time makes up a *Semibreve*.

In the fourth Bar of the *Fourths*, there is but one *Minim*, which is but half a *Semibreve*, the other half of the Time is made up by a *Minim Reft*, or *Paufe*. The like is in other of the Bars.

CHAP. IX.

Shewing how to Compare and Recon-
cile different Cliffs.

THE *Cliffs*, or *Signed Keys*, though as
to Character or Figure, they are
but three, 𝄢 , 𝄡 , 𝄞 ; yet as they are used
or set in several places of the Staff of Lines,
they are many more.

The *Tenor* Cliff being arbitrarily set on
any of the five Lines, is in effect five different Cliffs, in as much as it *five* several ways
alters the Names of the Lines and Spaces ;
the *Bass* Cliff also, whose proper Place is
the upper Line save one, being sometimes
set on the middle Line, is thereby in effect
two Cliffs ; so that in all, there be Eight :
This, tho' it be done for more convenient
pricking, is yet very inconvenient and troublesom, both for Voice and Instrument. A
general Remedy, by reducing all the Cliffs
to one (or three as one) was some years
ago ingeniously contrived, and publish'd,
by Mr. *Thomas Salmon*, of *Trinity-College* in
Oxford : Of this, I thought to have given a
brief

brief account, but have omitted it, judging the following Directions to be sufficient for the Voice.

Having by Practice perfected your self in the Rules of the foregoing Chapters, so that you can readily sing what you see prickt in the *Treble* and *Bass* Cliffs, (or at least in one of them;) your next business will be, to learn what to do, when you meet with the other Cliffs that you are a Stranger to. In this case, that you may the better understand the Grounds I go upon, it will be convenient, that you well know and remember the Half-Notes places, both with *Flats* and *Sharps*, and without, as they are taught, and represented to the Eye, in the five Scales of *Chap. VI.* For to name and sing true the Notes prick'd in one Cliff, as if they were in another, the only Requisite is, That the *Semitones* be either in their natural Order, or by help of *Flats* and *Sharps*, reduced to the same places of the Staff signed with a known Cliff as they are in the unknown.

When you meet with any thing prick'd in a strange Cliff, take this following Rule:

Reckon from the Cliff Line the seven Letters places, considering also the *Flats* or *Sharps*, if any be, and thereby find
be-

etween what Lines and Spaces the two
Semitones lye in the *Tenor* Cliff; which,
when you have obferved, confider what
Letters thofe Lines and Spaces are named by
in the Cliff you would reduce to, and accordingly, whether the *Semitones* be in the
fame places of the Staff, or not; if they be,
you have nothing to do, but name and fing
your Notes, as if they were in your defired
Cliff: But if the *Semitones*, one or both of
them, fall not in the fame places of the
Staff that they do in a known Cliff; confider what regular *Flats* or *Sharps*, placed on
the Staff, would reduce them to thofe places;
and then fuppofing the *Treble* or *Bafs* Cliff
fet to the Lines with fuch *Flats* or *Sharps*,
name and fing your Notes accordingly. An
Example or two will make this plainer
than many words. Take for inftance, a
Tenor and *Bafs*, as I find them prick'd in an
old *Pfalm* Book, to the 125th *Pfalm*.

1. For

1. For the *Tenor*, the ℭ Cliff standing upon the middle Line, that is the place of ℭ, and ℬe being *flat* under it, therefore is one half Note's place between ℬe and Lℭ, that is, between the lower Line save one, and the Space above it. Now in the *Treble* Cliff, that Line is ℭ, and the Space Lℭ, which are distant a whole Tone, or Note; and because no *Flat* or *Sharp* is usually placed on either of those Notes, therefore you cannot reduce and sing them in the *Treble* Cliff, but in the *Bass* only, wherein the lower Line save one is ℬ, and the Space above it ℭe, which two Notes are properly distant half a Tone.

Then for the other *Semitone* in the *Tenor*, it is betwixt Lℭ and ℱa; that is, (reckoning from the Cliff-Line) betwixt the upper Line save one, and the Space above it; which Line, in the *Bass*, is ℱa, and the Space ℭ, whose proper distance is a whole Tone, but

is

is reducible to a Semitone, by finging *Fa ſharp*; that is, half a Tone diſtant from ☉. So therefore, if you ſuppoſe or imagin the *Tenor* Cliff, with its *Flats*, ſtruck out, and the *Baſs* Cliff, with *Fa* ſigned *ſharp*, thus ſet inſtead of it, and ſing your Notes accordingly , D, D, Ce, B; LE, D, Ce, B; ☉, B, *&c.* you will ſing them as true, as if you had underſtood the *Tenor* Cliff, and ſung them as there , calling them, Ce, Ce, Be, La ; D, Ce, Be, La, *&c.*

2. The ſecond Tune , being the *Baſs* to the former, is prick'd in the *Baſs* Cliff; but the Cliff being ſet on the middle Line to take in the upper Notes , alters the Names of all the Lines and Spaces, and removes the *Semitones* : That you may therefore ſing the Notes true, you muſt reduce to the *Treble* Cliff, by the former Directions ; by which you will find, that they may be ſung true in the *Treble* Cliff, with B and E *flat*, and ſo they will be called, Be, Be, ME ; Be, ☉ ; Be, Ce, ☉ ; ☉, Be, *&c.*

Obſerve, That by whatever Names you call the Notes, for the Cliffs ſake, you muſt in ſinging of Parts , reckon the Cords in which

which the Parts begin, by the diſtance and
true names of the Notes, according to the
Cliff they are prick'd in. Thus in the former Example, if you reckon the diſtance
between the firſt Note of the *Tenor*, and the
firſt of the *Baſs*, as they are prick'd, you
will find, the Cord is a *Fifth*; *viz.* from ſ
in the *Baſs*, to C in the *Tenor*.

When you are perfect in the foregoing
Rule, you may your ſelf reduce, and ſing in
any Cliff whatever: But 'till then, and to
help you therein, here follows,

A T A B L E, *wherein the ſeveral
Cliffs are by the foregoing Rule reduced to the* Treble *and* Baſs.

I.

I I.

I I I.

III.

IV.

V.

VI.

VII.

This Table confifting of feven *Staves*,
hath in each of them all thofe *Cliffs* put together which have the *Semitones* in the fame
places. The firft *Cliff* in each Staff is the
Treble or *Bafs*, to which the reft are reduced.

The

The Use of the foregoing Table of Cliffs.

When you meet with any other *Cliff*, befides the *Treble* or *Bafs*, in their right places; Look that *Cliff*, as it is figned with *Flats*, &c. in the Table, and in the beginning of the fame Staff, you have the *Treble* or *Bafs* Cliff, fhewing how to name and fing your Notes.

Example.

In the former Example, the firft Tune is figned with the *Tenor* Cliff on the middle Line, and a *flat* on B, thus : Look for this *Cliff* in the Table, and you will find it in the feventh Staff, and at the beginning of the fame Staff is the *Bafs* Cliff, with f a figned *fharp* ; which fhews, that the Notes may be fung true, naming them as if they were in the *Bafs* Cliff, thus :

After

After this Difcourſe of Reconciling the *Cliffs*, that the convenience of the ſeven Notes Names made uſe of in this Eſſay, may the better appear, I ſhall here inſert

A TABLE, *wherein the Old Names of the Notes are compared with the New.*

La fa ſol la mi fa ſol la.

LE fâ G LA Be Ce D LE.

Mi fa ſol la fa ſol la mi.

LE fâ G LA Be Ce D LE

Fa ſol la mi fa ſol la fa.

ME fâ G LA Be Ce D ME.

Sol la mi fa ſol la fa ſol.

G LA B Ce D LE fâ G.

Sol la fa sol la mi fa sol.

G LA Be Ce D LE fa G.

La mi fa sol la fa sol la.

G LA Be Ce D ME fa G.

Fa sol la fa sol la mi fa.

*G LA Be Ce D LE fa G.

* This *Cliff* is reduced to the *Bass*, and the *Notes* named accordingly.

The *Cliff* signed with *Sharps*.

La mi fa sol la fa sol la.

LE fa G LA B Ce D LE.

Sol la fa sol la mi fa sol.

LE fa G LA B C D LE.

In this Table, the old Names being set over the Staff, and the new ones under, it will by inspection appear,　　　1. That

1. That the seven Letters, or new Names or the Notes, have but two different places, (with their *Octaves*,) *viz.* as in the *Treble* and *Bass* Cliffs, to which, all the rest are reduced.

2. That *Mi* (and therewith the other Names) in the old way, is shifted into *seven* different places (marked with *black Notes*); and accordingly, before a person in that way can be Master of all the *Cliffs*, or indeed of the *Treble* and *Bass* only, he must learn to sing *Mi* in every Line and Space of the Staff.

3. That if the Cliffs have *Sharps* annexed, each Cliff severally will have *five* different places of *Mi*, if it be placed as it ought, *viz.* in F, when F is signed *sharp* at the beginning of the Staff; and in C, when F and C are both *sharp*: But I never met with any Book that shewed where to set *Mi* in case of *Sharps*, though Tunes are sometimes prick'd that way, as well for Voice as Instrument, and then, if they alter not the place of *Mi*, they must sing contrary to their own Rule, in singing a whole Note next under *Fa*.

By what hath been said, may be understood how to transfer Lessons from one *Cliff*

to

to another, and (for the Voice) from one Key to another; the only Requisite being, that the *Semitones* be in their right places.

CHAP. X.

Containing Pfalm Tunes, *with Directions how to Sing them.*

1. OF all the Ufes of *Music*, that in Divine Things is moft Excellent and Honourable; whereby it becomes inftrumental to the celebrating of the Praifes of Almighty God, the Author of *Being, Order,* and *Harmony.* 'Tis true, the Melody of a devout Heart is that which is moft pleafant in the Ears of God, without which, all other Mufic is but Jarr and Difcord; yet when both are well conjoyned, the Confort is more full, and the Affections more eafily excited. Heaven it felf is fet forth to our Apprehenfions by the joyful Melody of *Hallelujahs,* and Songs of *Praife*; and 'tis furely one of the moft Heavenly Exercifes on Earth, when good *Chriftians,* with Heart and Voice, concordantly Praife their Maker, Redeemer, and Comforter.

But

But this Confideration including more things than are proper here to be fpoken of, I fhall therefore in the next place, after a few Directions, prefent you with a Collection of Tunes fitted to the ufual *Metres*, wherein *Pfalms* and *Hymns* are compofed.

2. There be two forts of finging, the one is common and ufual in all places, *viz*. when all the Company fing in *Unifon*, or the fame Tune; the other kind is, when they fing in Parts, two, three, or more; that is, when the Company is divided into fo many Parts, and each Part fings a diftinct Tune; yet fo compofed in Concordance, that being fung together, they yield a moft delightful Harmony, moft befitting grave and folemn Matters. This latter kind of finging being not fo commonly underftood, is more rarely ufed: I fhall therefore give fome Examples of it, with Directions how to perform it.

In all Tunes or Leffons confifting of Parts, one Part is the *Bafs*, (fo called, becaufe it is the *Bafis*, Foundation, or Ground-work, to the other Part or Parts, and on which the Harmony is built:) They that fing this Part, muft have deep, ftrong, and big Voices; in it, the Notes move for the moft part by

F 3   Leaps;

Leaps; but in the upper Part, their Movement is more by degrees.

Here two things muſt be obſerv'd: Firſt, That you begin at a convenient pitch of Voice for reaching all the Notes; for which purpoſe, you muſt count how many Notes in compaſs the Parts take in, that you may ſo begin, as to reach them without ſqueeking or grumbling. Secondly, You muſt obſerve on what Notes the ſeveral Parts begin, and in what Concords, that you may ſet out accordingly.

3. In *Anthems*, and ſome *Hymns*, where there be Reſts, and Notes of different Time, it is alſo neceſſary to *keep Time* by the motion of *Hand* or *Foot*; but this is needleſs in the ordinary *Pſalm* Tunes, becauſe the Motion is ſlow, and for the moſt part the Notes go one for one.

An Example of two Parts.

In this Example, the firſt thing to be conſidered, is the Compaſs of the Notes, which
if you reckon from the higheſt Note of the
Treble, Be, to the loweſt of the *Baſs,* Fâ,
is eleven Notes, *viz.* three above the firſt
of the *Treble,* and ſeven below it; therefore
muſt the *Treble* Part begin Fâ high, having
but three Degrees higher to go : The *Baſs*
begins at Fâ, an *Octave* below the *Treble.*
Having begun, they move on Note for Note,
in various Concord, to the Cloſe.

Note : That the upper Fâ of the *Baſs* is
ſuppoſed to be in *Uniſon* the ſame Tune with
the lower Fâ on the *Treble ;* and therefore is
the Compaſs reckoned but eleven *Notes,*
which otherwiſe would have been eighteen ;
too much compaſs for the Voice. The like
muſt be underſtood in the Examples following.

One thing more to be conſidered in theſe,
and all other Tunes, is the *Air* or *Humour* of
the Key in which they are ſet, to wit, whe-

ther it be *sharp* or *flat*. The Key in Lessons, if many Parts, is known by the *Bass*, the last Note of that Part being always the Key. In other single Tunes, the last Note is on the Key. When you know the Key, consider the Third above it, whether it be the greater or lesser Third; if it be the greater Third, (or two whole Tones) then is the Key *sharp*; and if it be the lesser Third, (or a Tone and an half) then is the Key *flat*.

The knowledge of this, gives you to understand something of the Air of a Tune, before you begin to learn it. A Flat Key is *soft* and *sweet*; a Sharp Key is more *lively* and *chearful*; yet so, as that to these Qualities in both, the *Movement* and *Time* of the Notes do also more or less concur.

When you have observ'd the Key, begin thereat, and marking where the *Half Notes* lye, rise with your Voice eight Notes to the *Octave* above, and by the same Steps descend. If you do this heedfully two or three times, before you begin to learn a Tune, you will be the readier at it.

If your Tune rise not more than *six Notes* above the Key, you then need only to begin your *six Notes*, so that the Key it self be always either the *fifth* or *sixth* Note: For which, take this RULE.

RULE.

Every Sharp Key *is the Sixth, or lowest of* Six Notes ; *and every* Flat Key *is the Fifth Note of the* Six.

Here follow two Examples to apply this *Rule.*

Example I.

First Staff.

Second Staff.

The last Note of the Tune is 𝔊, which is the Key : From 𝔊 to 𝔅 is two whole Notes, and therefore is the Key *sharp.* Begin your *six* therefore, so that 𝔊 be the last, that is, at
LE,

LE, and sing, LE, D, Ce, B, LA, G, and
then backward, G, LA, B, Ce, D, LE, two
or three times, and then proceed to the
Tune.

In the first Staff, you have a Pfalm Tune
for an Example, which confisting much of
Leaps, I have in the second Staff put the
intermediate Steps in *Quavers*, or fhorter
Notes: So that if you fing the second Staff
firft, giving the Notes their due time, it
will be eafie to fing afterward the Tune in
the firft Staff. The like you may do your
felf by other.

Example II.

First Staff.

Second Staff.

In

In this Example, the laſt Note is 𝔊 ; from whence to Be *flat*, is a Note and half, therefore is the Key *flat*. Begin your *Six* at D, ſo will 𝔊 be the *fifth* Note. After you have ſung all *ſix*, begin again, and ſtop at 𝔊, which five Notes give you the Air of a *flat* Key.

Sing the ſecond Staff firſt, and then the firſt, which is a Pſalm Tune.

AN EASIE
PRAXIS
For Exerciſe of the
Foregoing RULES:
BEING

A Collection of *Pſalm* Tunes in Parts, prick'd in ſeveral *Keys*, with the Varieties of *Flats* and *Sharps*, for Example ſake ; the Compaſs of the Parts ſuch as will not exceed the reach of ordinary Voices.

The Words are (for the moſt part) taken out of Mr. Patrick's *Verſion.*

First Treble, *or* **C. Tune.** *Pfal.* **1.** **Sharp Key.**

THe man is bleſt, who hath not bent, to wicked read his ear;

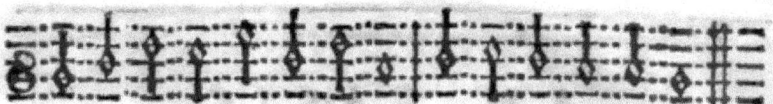

Baſs.

nor led his life as ſinners do, nor ſate in ſcorners chair.

Second Treble, *or* **Middle Part.**

THe man is bleſt, who hath not bent, to wicked read his ear;

nor led his life as ſinners do, nor ſate in ſcorners chair.

Common Tune.　　　*Pſalm 23.*　　　Flat Key.

My Shepherd is the living Lord, nothing therefore I need;

Bass.

In paſtures fair, with waters calm, he ſets me forth to feed.

Middle Part.

My Shepherd is the living Lord, nothing therefore I need;

in paſtures fair, with waters calm, he ſets me forth to feed.

Common Tune.   Psalm 37.   Flat Key.

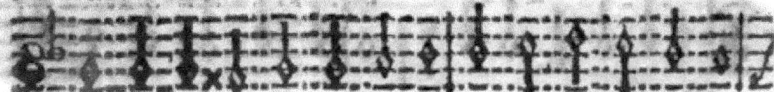

Let none be troubled to behold, the wicked's prosp'rous state;
Bass.

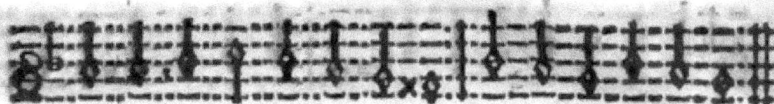

nor by their good success grow bold, their crimes to i-mi-tate.

Middle Part.

Let none be troubled to behold, the wicked's prosp'rous state;

nor by their good success grow bold, their crimes to i-mi-tate.

Treble.   Psalm 39.

Lord, teach me when my end, and days I have to live, I view;

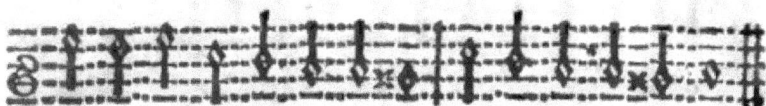

Bass.

to know my self and them, how frail I am, and they are few.

Middle Part.

Lord, teach me when my end, and days I have to live, I view;

to know my self and them, how frail I am, and they are few.

Treble.　　　　　*Pfalm* 40.

'TIS good with patience to attend, and on the Lord re--ly;

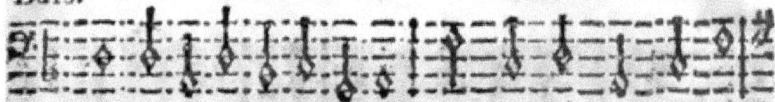

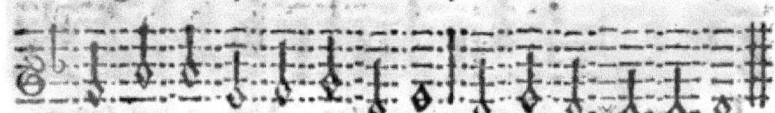

Bass.

when　other fuccours fail'd, to him I pray'd, who heard my cry.

Middle Part:

'T IS good with patience to attend, and on the Lord rely;

when other fuccours fail'd, to him I pray'd, who heard my cry.

Or the *Middle Part* may be prick'd thus:

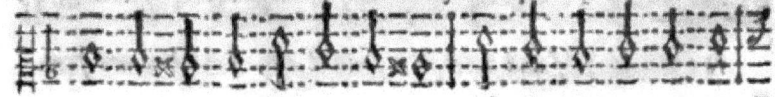

☞ Begin in *Unifon* with the *Common Tune*, and fing the
Notes as if in the *Treble Cliff* Proper; L☛, L☛, ☉, L☛, &c.

[81]

Common Tune.　　*Pfalm 95.*

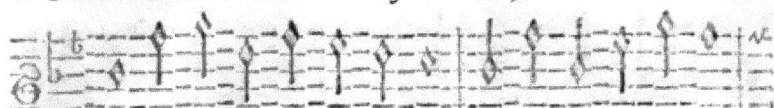

Come let us with u-ni-ted joys, to God our voices raife;

Bafs.

with thankful hearts before him come, and loudly fing his praife.

Middle Part.

Come let us with u-ni-ted joys, to God our voices raife;

with thankful hearts before him come, and loudly fing his praife.

G

[82]

Common Tune. Psalm 51.

BEhold, O Lord, my sinful Soul to thee for mercy flies;

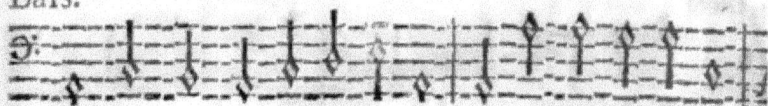

Bass.

thy mercy boundless is, blot out all mine i—ni-qui-ties.

Middle Part.

BEhold, O Lord, my sinful Soul to thee for mercy flies;

thy mercy boundless is, blot out all mine i—ni-qui-ties.

The former Tune prick'd on C *Cliff*, to
exercise *Reduction* according to *Chap. IX.*
The *Bass* is the same as before; but the
other Parts must be sung in G *Cliff*, with
Be and ME *flat.* The *Common Tune* be-
gins an Eight above the *Bass*, and the
Middle Part a *flat* Third above the
Common Tune.

Behold, O Lord, my sinful Soul to thee for mercy flies;
Bass.

thy mercy boundless is, blot out all mine i——ni··qui·ties.

Middle Part.

Behold, O Lord, my sinful Soul to thee for mercy flies;

thy mercy boundless is, blot out all mine i——ni··qui·ties.

Here follow long Tunes of Eight Lines
to a Staff, for the Metre of the
First Pſalm.

Treble.   Pſalm 119.

BLeſt is the man, whoſe blameleſs life the law of God directs;

Baſs.

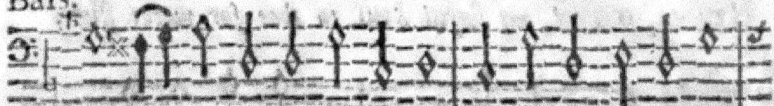

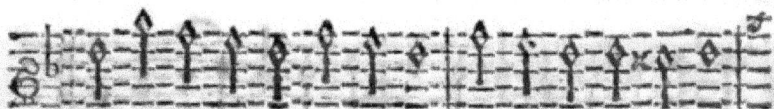

who keeps his precepts, and whoſe heart to ſerve the Lord affects:

They never wil-ful--ly tranſgreſs, who to thoſe paths repair;

thou, Lord, haſt charged us to keep all thy commands with care.

Middle Part.

B Leſt is the man, whoſe blameleſs life the law of God directs;

who keeps his precepts, and whoſe heart, to ſerve the Lord affects:

They never wil-ful--ly tranſgreſs, who to thoſe paths repair;

thou, Lord, haſt charged us to keep all thy commands with care.

Common Tune.   Psalm 84.

How beauteous is the place, where thou thy presence, Lord, dost grant

Bass.

Oh! how I long t'approach thy courts, impatient of restraint!

Oh happy men! that may frequent thine house to praise thee still

whose trust is in thine aid, whose heart devout affections fill.

Middle Part.

How beauteous is the place, where thou thy presence, Lord, dost grant!

Oh! how I long t'approach thy courts, impatient of restraint!

Oh happy men! that may frequent thine house to praise thee still;

whose trust is in thine aid, whose heart devout affections fill.

G 4.

An *Hymn* taken out of the *Revelations*:

By Mr. *Patrick*.

Treble.

All ye that serve the Lord his name, see that ye ce- le-brate;

Bass.

And ye that fear him sing a--loud, his praise both small and great:

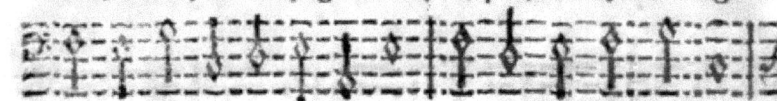

O thou great ruler of the world, thy works our wonders raise;

thou blessed King of saints, how true, and righteous are thy ways!

Mean.

ALL ye that serve the Lord his name, see that ye celebrate,

and ye that praise him sing aloud, his praise both small and great:

O thou great ruler of the world, thy works our wonders raise;

thou blessed King of saints, how true, and righteous are thy ways!

II. (Name,
Who would not fear and praise thy
Thou only holy one! (whom
The world will worship thee, to
Thy judgments are made known:
Most holy, holy, holy Lord,
Almighty is thy name;
Which was before all time, and is,
And shall be still the same.

III.
All glory, pow'r, and honour, thou
Art worthy to receive; (made,
For all things by thy pow'r were
And by thy pleasure live:
To thee of right, O Lamb of God,
Riches and pow'r belong;
Wisdom and honour, glory, strength,
And ev'ry praising Song.

IV.
Thou, as our Sacrifice, wast slain,
And by thy precious blood,
From ev'ry Tongue and Nation, hast
Redeem'd us unto God
Blessing and honour, glory, pow'r,
By all in earth and heav'n;
To him that sits upon the Throne,
And to the Lamb be giv'n.

[90]

An Example of Four Parts.

Common Tune.   *Pfalm* 105.

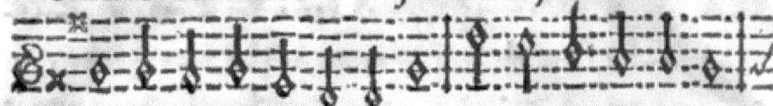

O Let us all give thanks to God, and call upon his name;
Bass.

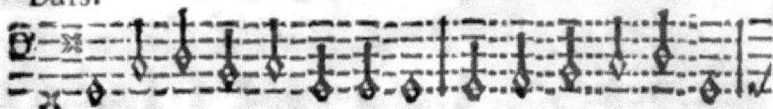

his gracious and his mighty works, to all the world proclaim :

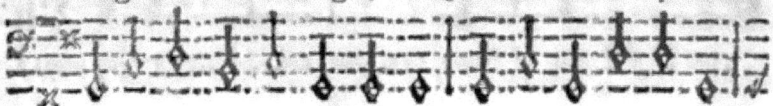

Let us in songs, and sacred hymns, our great Cre-a-tor bless;

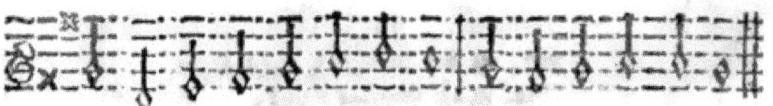

and what his pow'rful hand hath wrote, our joyful tongues express.

First Mean.

O let us all give thanks to God, and call upon his name;

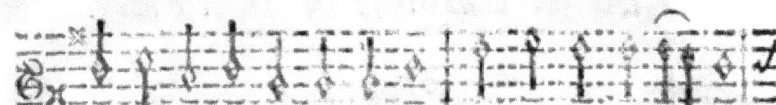

his gracious and his mighty works, to all the world proclaim:

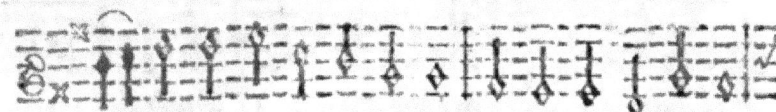

Let us in Songs, and sacred hymns, our great Cre-a-tor bless;

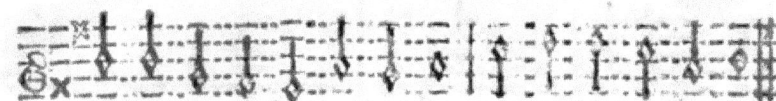

and what his pow'rful hand hath wrote, our joyful tongues expreſs.

Second Mean.

O let us all give thanks to God, and call upon his name;

his graciou and his mighty works, to all the world proclaim:

Let us in songs, and sacred hymns, our great Cre-a-tor b'ess;

and what his pow'rful hand hath wrote, our joyful tongues ex-preſs.

Tunes for the Metre of the 100th Psalm, Eight Syllables to a Line.

Another Example of Four Parts.

Treble.   **Psalm 100.**

ALl people that on earth do dwell, sing to the Ld. with chearful voice;

Bass.

him serv with fear, his praise forth tell, com ye befor him & rejoyce.

First Mean.

All people, &c.

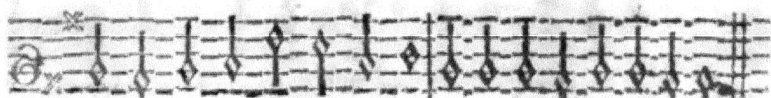

Second Mean,

All people, &c.

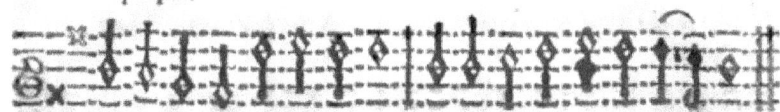

Treble. *Pſalm* 1 39.

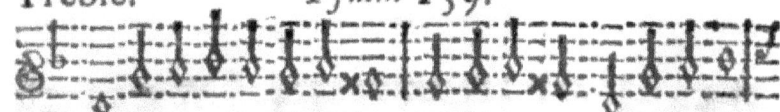

Lord, when I have to do with thee, in vain I ſeek to be conceal'd;

Baſs.

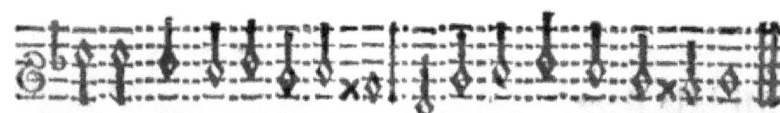

thou know'ſt me perfeſtly, to thee my very thoughts are all reveal'd.

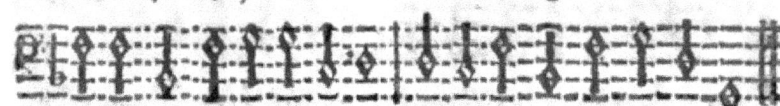

Mean.

Lord, when I have to do with thee, in vain I ſeek to be conceal'd;

thou know'ſt me perfeſtly, to thee my very thoughts are all reveal'd.

Treble. *Pſalm* 1.

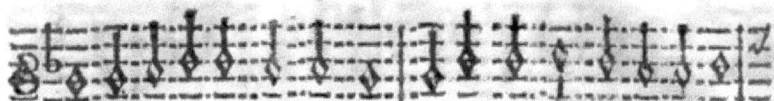

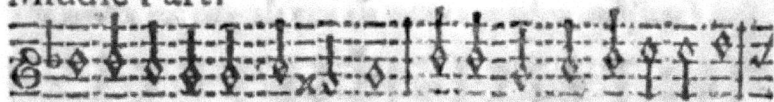

B Leſt is the man, whoſe vertuous ſteps no wicked counſels lead aſide ;

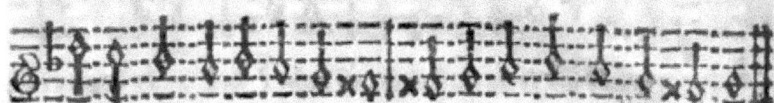

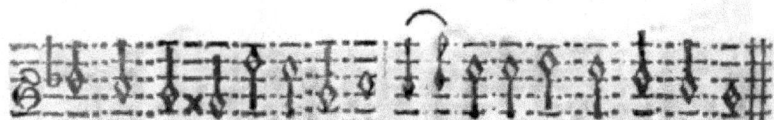

Baſs.

nor ſtands in ſinners way, nor ſits where God & goodneſs men deride.

Middle Part:

B Leſt is the man, whoſe vertuous ſteps no wicked counſels lead aſide;

nor ſtands in ſinners way, nor ſits where God & goodneſs men deride.

[95]

Common Tune.   Pfalm 103.

Blefs thou the Ld. my foul, his name, let all the pow'rs within me blefs;
Bafs.

O let not his paft favours lye for-got-ten in unthankfulnefs!

Middle Part.

Blefs thou the Ld. my foul, his name, let all the pow'rs within me blefs;

O let not his paft favours lye forgotten in unthankfulnefs!

Treble.   The 113th Pfalm. Tune.

TE fervants of th'eternal king, to God your chearful praifes fing,

Bafs.

whofe name be bleft for evermore. His goodnefs over all is great,

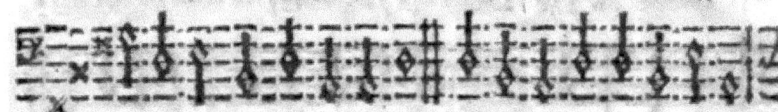

where e're the fun does rife or fet; fince all are bleft, let all adore.

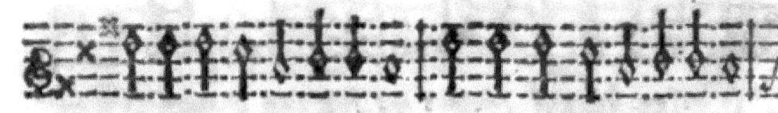

O're all the earth the L. does reign, & heav'ns too narrow to contain

his glories that are infinite. Let not poor borow'd greatness dare

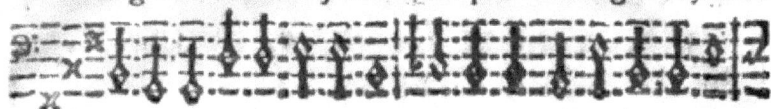

with his perfections to compare, who dwells in un-cre-a-ted light:

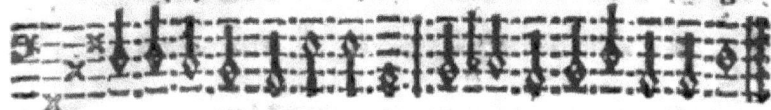

Middle Part:

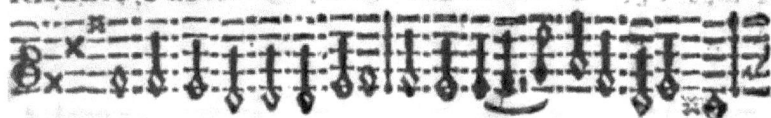

Ye Servants, &c.

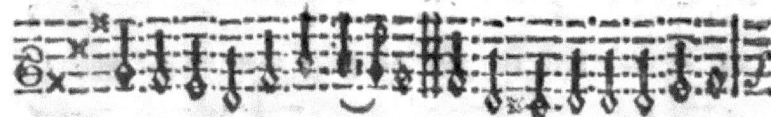

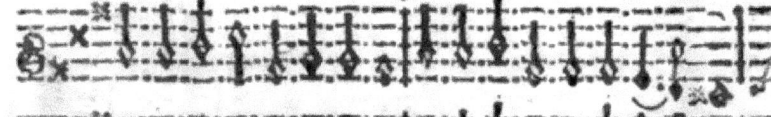

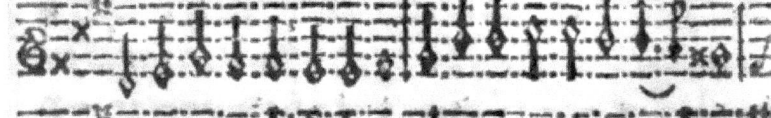

H

[96]

In the following Tune, the *Treble* and *Middle Parts* are prick'd in the C *Cliff*, and left without Directions, that the Learner may try his Skill in *Reduction*, by the Rules in the Ninth Chapter.

Com. Tune.   *The* 148*th Pfalm Tune.*

To laud the Heav'nly King, let all their Voices raife;
Baſs.

Ye Angels, firſt be--gin the great Cre--a--tor's praiſe:

Let Sun and Moon, and ev'ry Star, his Glory ſhew that's brighter far.

Middle Part.

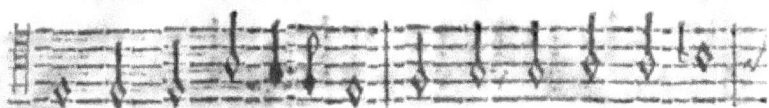

To laud the Heav'nly King, let all their Voices raise;

Ye Angels, first be---gin the great Cre--a--tor's praise:

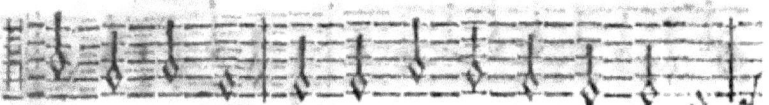

Let Sun and Moon, and ev'--ry star, his Glo---ry shew,

that's brighter far.

Treble. *To the Metre of Psalm 25.*

I lift my heart to thee, my God and guide most just;

Bass.

now suffer me to take no shame, for in thee do I trust.

Middle Part.

I lift my heart to thee, my God and guide most just;

now suffer me to take no shame, for in thee do I trust.

The Notes of the foregoing *Tune* are usually broken or divided, and they are
better so sung, as is here prick'd.

I lift my heart to thee,

my God and guide most just;

now suf—fer me to take no shame,

for in thee do I trust.

Another Tune for the Metre of Psalm 25.

Treble.

Awake, my Soul, look up! thy best affections raise;

Bass.

With Hallelujahs sing aloud, the great Jehovah's praise.

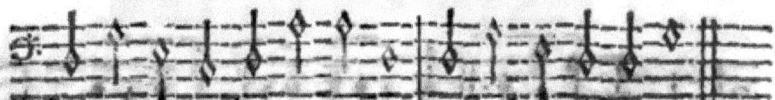

Middle Part:

Awake, my Soul, look up! thy best Af---fections raise;

with Hal-le-lu-jahs sing aloud, the great Jehovah's praise.

Angels

Angels and Saints all rest,
  The Heavenly Hosts above,
There cease not day and night to sing
  The Songs of Praise and Love.

The Heav'ns declare the Pow'r
  And Glory of the Lord;
Their useful Light and influence,
  Large Praises do afford.

The Air and Earth below;
  All things that we behold,
Eternal Pow'r and Godhead shew,
  And unseen things unfold.

How great and manifold
  Are all thy works, O Lord!
In Wisdom hast thou made them all,
  By thy most pow'rful Word.

But, Lord, what Tongue of Man
  Or Angels can declare,
The Wonders of thy Love and Grace,
  Which in Christ Jesus are?

All we, like wand'ring Sheep,
  From thee were gone aside;
Thou sen'st thy Son to seek and save,
  Who came, and for us dy'd.

Glory to God on high!
  On Earth Good Will and Peace;
Let Heav'n and Earth give praise to God,
  And praising, never cease.

A Tune

A Tune for the Long Metre of Ten Syllables to a Line.

2 Parts. Pſal. 67. Mr. Goodridg's Tranſlation.

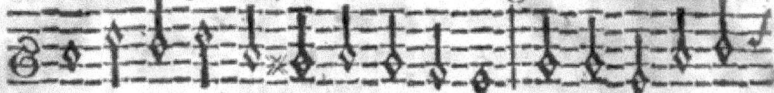

BE merciful, O God, chaſe away night; and bleſs us with the

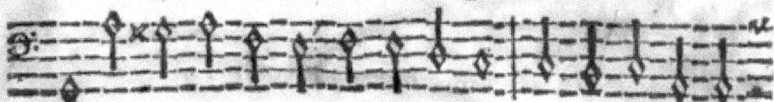

viſion of thy Light; that un--to all the earth thy way be known,

thy u--ni--ver-ſal glad Sa'--va--ti--on.

Moſt of the *Pſalms* in this Metre, with more Tunes to them, you may have in Mr. *Goodridges* late Verſion.

FINIS.

www.ingramcontent.com/pod-product-compliance
Lightning Source LLC
Chambersburg PA
CBHW030627270326
41927CB00007B/1335